Who Makes Our Laws?

Table of Contents

Getting Started 2
City 4
State 8
Nation 12
Index 16

by Carol K. Lindeen

Getting Started

Can you think of some rules at your school? How about always walking in the hallways? The principal at your school doesn't make this rule to spoil your fun. People make rules because they want to keep you safe. Rules help to protect you.

Laws are special rules that all of us must follow. Laws help to keep us safe. Do you know who makes our laws? The **government** does. The government is made up of people who make or change our laws.

The Constitution lists the very first laws made by the U.S. government.

Your town or city has a government. So does your state. And all states must follow the laws of our country, the United States. Let's read about how our government works.

City

Most cities or towns have a group of leaders called a *council*. Both men and women can be on the council. Council members are usually elected, or chosen, by the people. To elect someone we **vote** for that person.

In most cities, voters also elect a leader called the *mayor*. The mayor is usually in charge of the city. It is kind of like the way a school principal is in charge of the school.

The mayor has meetings with the city council to talk about important things. The meetings usually happen in a building called *city hall*.

The mayor and city council members are only the leaders in their own city. They are not in charge of other places. Also, the laws in one city might not be the same as the laws in another city.

City laws may tell us about safe places to park our cars. They may help to make sure our sidewalks are kept clean. City laws even help keep pets healthy and safe.

State

Each state has its own government. In each state, voters elect people from their area to work in the state **legislature**. The legislature is a group of people who make laws for the whole state.

The leader of the state is the governor. The **governor** can say yes or no to laws that the legislature passes. The governor also chooses other people who help make important decisions for the state.

Each state has a city called the *capital.* The state's main government offices are in a special building in the capital city. The governor and other state workers work there.

The governor and the legislature are only in charge of the laws in their state. They don't make laws for other states. Do you know the name of your state's governor?

State laws help to protect all the people in the state. They help to keep our highways safe. They help to keep our air and water clean. State laws also help to make sure our schools are good places to learn.

Nation

All states must follow our nation's laws. Men and women elected from each state make up a group called the **Congress**. Congress makes our nation's laws.

The leader of the United States is called the **president**. The president is elected to work for four years in a row. Then the voters can elect a new president. Sometimes voters choose to keep the same president for four more years.

The White House

Our nation's capital is Washington, D.C. One of the most important buildings there is called the **White House**. This is where the president lives and works.

Our president makes important choices for our nation with help from Congress. Sometimes they alter, or change, old laws. Sometimes they make new laws, if they think that is best for our nation.

Our nation's laws help us in many important ways. These laws work together with our city laws and state laws. They help us know what we must do to be good citizens of the United States.

Index

capital, 9, 13

city(ies), 3, 4, 6, 7, 9, 15

city hall, 5

Congress, 12, 15

council, 4–6

government, 2, 3, 8, 9

governor, 8–10

law(s), 2, 3, 6–8, 10, 12, 15

legislature, 8, 10

mayor, 4–6

president, 12, 13, 15

state(s), 3, 8–10, 12, 15

town(s), 3, 4

United States, 3, 12, 15

voters, 4, 8, 12

White House, 13